PHONICS LAND

BOOK 3

Long Vowels

YBM

Contents

Phonics Land Book 3 Unit Plan

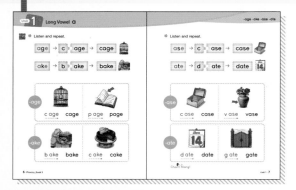

Letters and Sounds
New target combinations of sounds and related words are introduced with pictures.

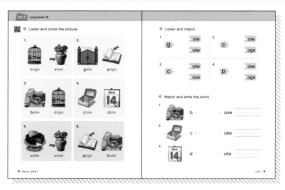

Practice 1
Children practice listening to words with the target sounds. They also practice identifying and writing the target sounds.

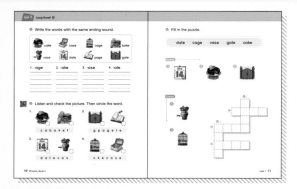

Practice 2
Children practice listening and writing the target words.

Activity
Children practice writing the target words in the activity.

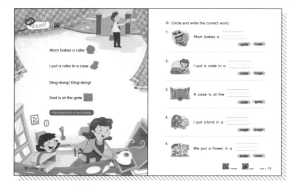

Let's Read!
Children further practice the target words by reading a simple story.

Practice 3
Children confirm their understanding of the target words by writing the words in simple sentences.

Review & Challenge
The Review provides practice of the materials from the previous four units by using a variety of exercises for the target sounds of letters and words.
The Challenge provides a chance to review the entire book. It reinforces students' phonics skills with various exercises and a test.

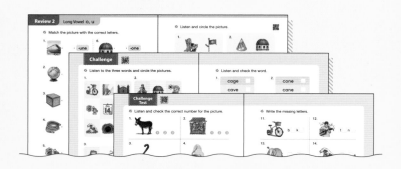

Special Features

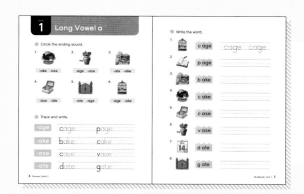

❂ Workbook ❂

Students review what they learned in class.
This can be used as homework or further practice.

❂ How to use QR codes ❂

Scan QR codes on the content pages, then you can use all of the listening sounds and flash animations, such as chants, stories, and listening questions.

e-learning — Scan e-learning QR codes, then you can use e-learning for self-study.

game — Scan game QR codes, then you can enjoy the phonics games.

⋅ Note for Teachers ⋅

The ultimate goal of the book is to help students be able to read and write words even if they encounter a new word. Therefore, students should be encouraged to listen and to identify the sounds of the letters, not to memorize the spellings of the words.

✿ Listen and repeat.

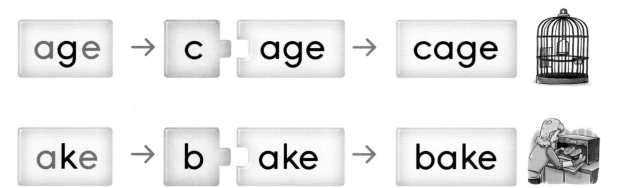

age → c age → cage

ake → b ake → bake

-age

c age   cage

p age   page

-ake

b ake   bake

c ake   cake

Listen and repeat.

ase → c ase → case 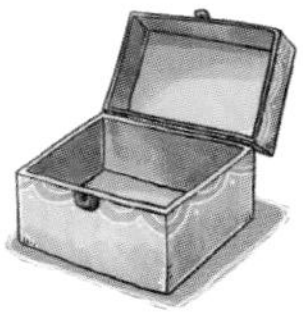

ate → d ate → date 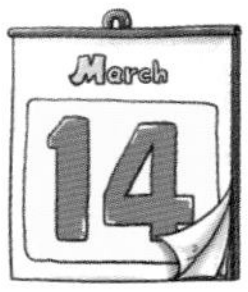

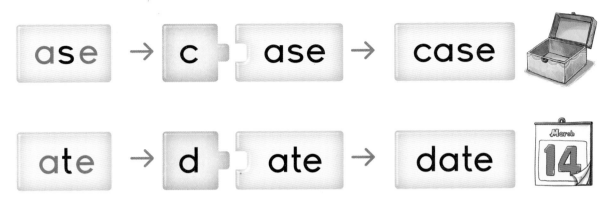

-ase

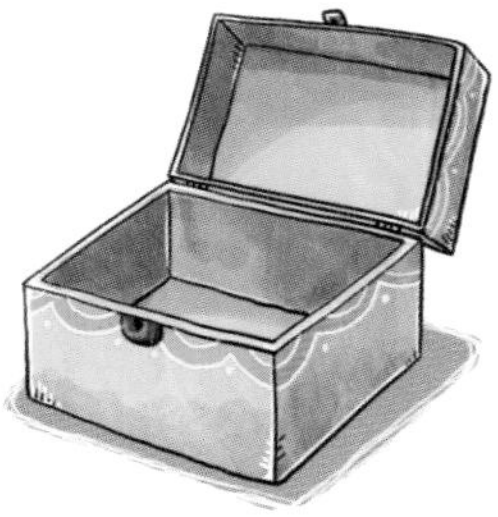

c ase → case

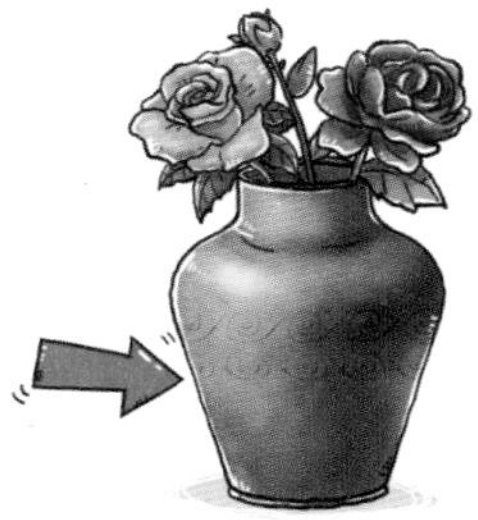

v ase → vase

-ate

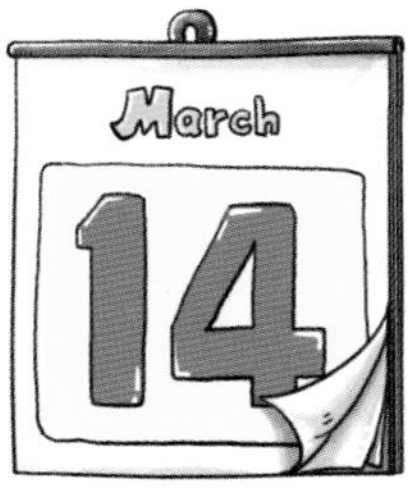

d ate → date

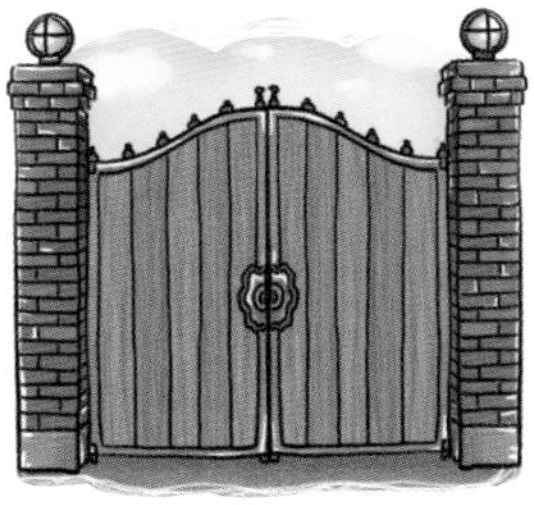

g ate → gate

Chant Along!

🌸 Listen and circle the picture.

1.
cage   vase

2.
gate   page

3.
bake   cage

4.
case   date

5.
cake   vase

6.
page   bake

✿ Listen and match.

1.

g

ate

ake

2.

c

ate

age

3.

c

ake

ase

4.

p

ase

age

✿ Match and write the word.

1.

b •

• ase _____

2.

c •

• ake _____

3.

d •

• ate _____

✿ Write the words with the same ending sound.

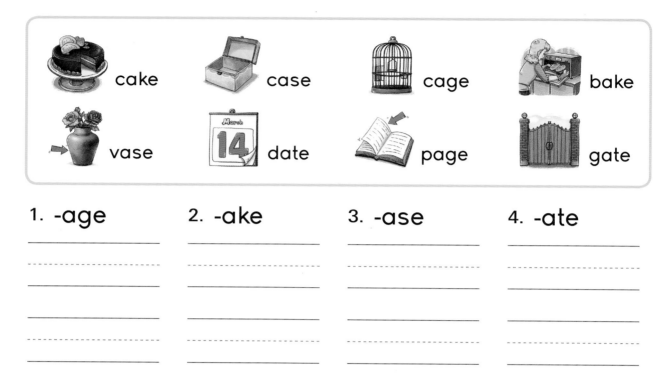

cake   case   cage   bake

vase   date   page   gate

1. -age

2. -ake

3. -ase

4. -ate

✿ Listen and check the picture. Then circle the word.

1.

c a b a k e f

2.

g p a g e t e

3.

d a t e v a s

4.

c k e c a s e

✿ Fill in the puzzle.

date   cage   vase   gate   cake

Across →

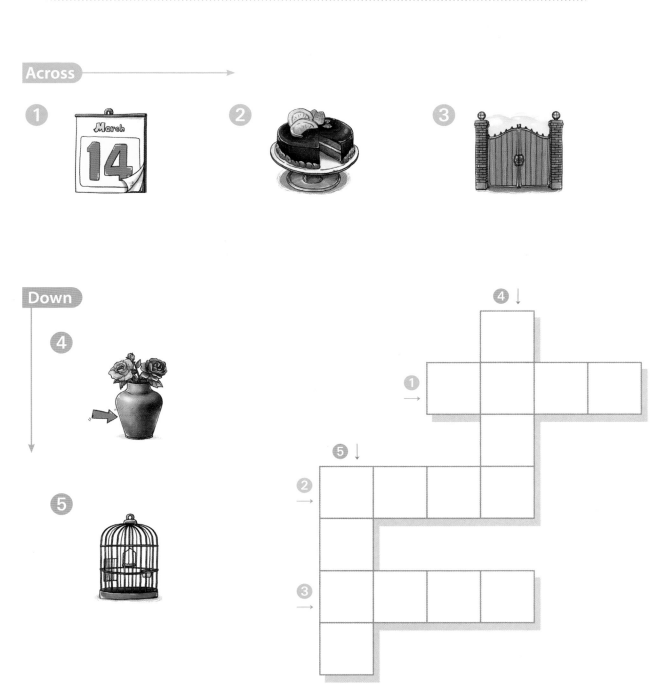

Down ↓

Mom bakes a cake .

I put a cake in a case .

Ding-dong! Ding-dong!

Dad is at the gate .

• Place the sticker on the shadow.

❀ Circle and write the correct word.

1. Mom bakes a _____ .

gate   cake

2. I put a cake in a _____ .

case   cage

3. A case is at the _____ .

date   gate

4. I put a bird in a _____ .

cage   page

5. We put a flower in a _____ .

bake   vase

 e-learning   game   Unit 1 · **13**

✿ Listen and repeat.

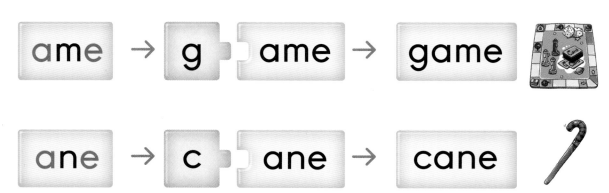

ame → g ame → game

ane → c ane → cane

-ame

g ame   game   n ame   name

-ane

c ane   cane   l ane   lane

✿ Listen and repeat.

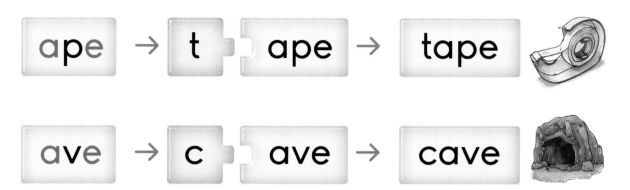

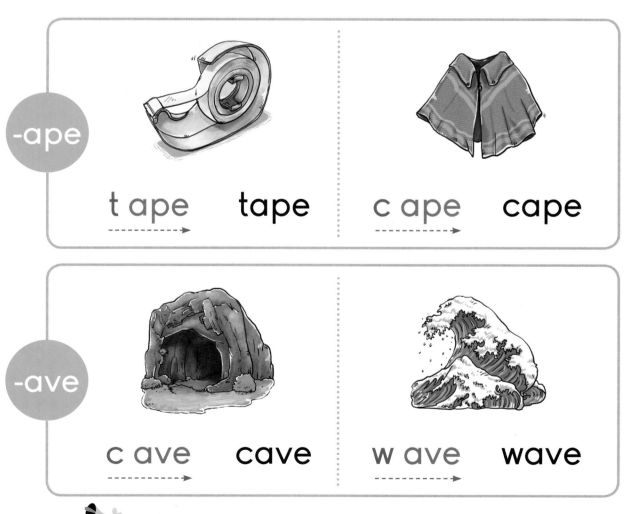

-ape

t ape   tape   c ape   cape

-ave

c ave   cave   w ave   wave

Chant Along!

🌸 Listen and circle the picture.

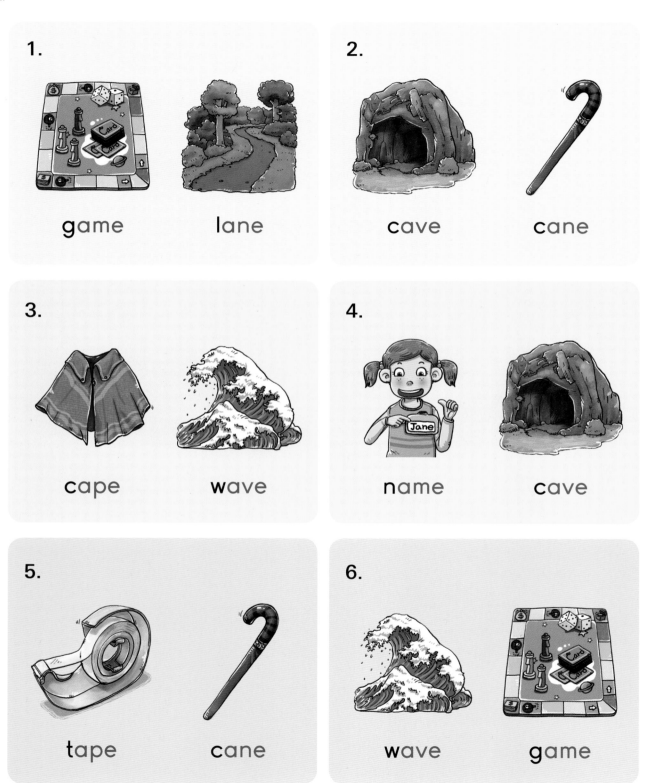

1.

game　　　lane

2.

cave　　　cane

3.

cape　　　wave

4.

name　　　cave

5.

tape　　　cane

6.

wave　　　game

✿ Listen and match.

1.

g

ape

ame

2.

l

ane

ave

3.

w

ape

ave

4.

n

ame

ane

✿ Match and write the word.

1.

t •

• ave

_____

2.

c •

• ane

_____

3.

l •

• ape

_____

✿ Write the words with the same ending sound.

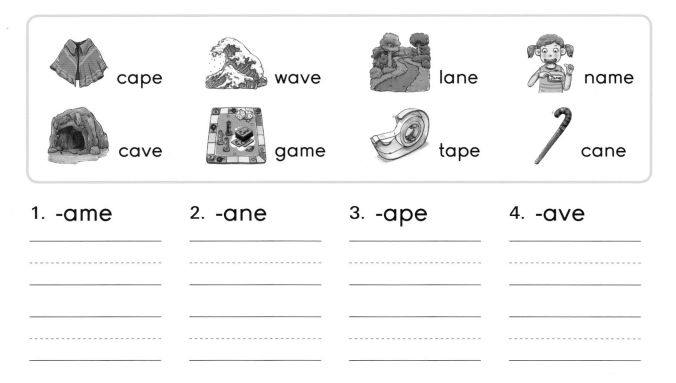

cape wave lane name

cave game tape cane

1. -ame
_____
- - - - - - - - - - - - - - -
_____
_____
- - - - - - - - - - - - - - -
_____

2. -ane
_____
- - - - - - - - - - - - - - -
_____
_____
- - - - - - - - - - - - - - -
_____

3. -ape
_____
- - - - - - - - - - - - - - -
_____
_____
- - - - - - - - - - - - - - -
_____

4. -ave
_____
- - - - - - - - - - - - - - -
_____
_____
- - - - - - - - - - - - - - -
_____

 ✿ Listen and check the picture. Then circle the word.

1.

c a n e n i n

2.

t h w a v e p

3.

c v e n a m e

4.

p l a n e c a

❀ Write the correct word under each picture.

cane   wave   name   tape   lane   cape

There is a bear with a cape  .

What's your name ?

Come out of the cave .

Let's play a game .

• Place the sticker on the shadow.

✿ Circle and write the correct word.

1. There is a bear with a _____ .

   cave   cape

2. There is a monkey with a _____ .

   lane   cane

3. A fox comes out of a _____ .

   wave   cave

4. What's your _____ ?

   name   tape

5. We play a _____ .

   cape   game

✿ Listen and repeat.

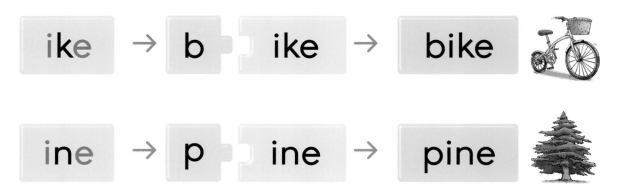

ike → b ike → bike

ine → p ine → pine

-ike

b ike   **bike**

m ike   **mike**

-ine

p ine   **pine**

n ine   **nine**

✿ Listen and repeat.

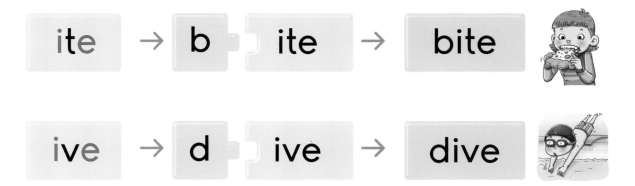

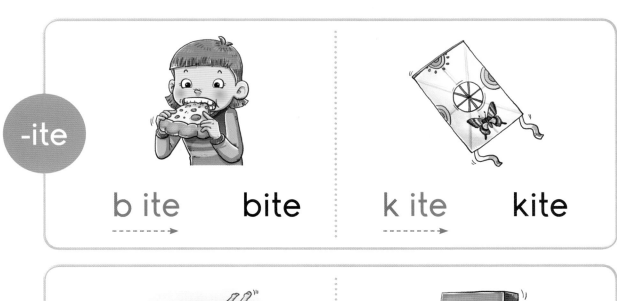

-ite

b ite → bite

k ite → kite

-ive

d ive → dive

f ive → five

Chant Along!

✿ Listen and circle the correct picture and the rhyme.

1.

-ike -ite

2.

-ine -ive

3.

-ike -ine

4.

-ive -ite

5.

-ine -ike

6.

-ike -ive

✿ Check the rhyme and write the word.

1. ☐ ive   ☐ ite   d_____

2. ☐ ine   ☐ ike   m_____

3. ☐ ite   ☐ ive   b_____

4. ☐ ine   ☐ ite   n_____

5. ☐ ike   ☐ ite   b_____

❉ Match the pictures with the same ending sound.
Then write.

1.

2.

3.

4.

 ❉ Listen and write the missing letters. Then match.

1. __ i __ e

2.  __ i __ e

3. __ i __ e

4. __ i __ e

✿ Find and circle the word in the puzzle. Then write the word.

1.

bike

2.

3.

4.

5.

6.

c	b	i	t	e	p	u
p	i	h	m	i	v	m
i	k	i	t	e	q	i
n	e	b	x	g	i	k
e	w	f	d	i	v	e

There are nine **9** kites in the pine.

Let's get a kite  .

There are five bikes under the pine 🌲 .

Let's get a bike 🚲 .

- Place the sticker on the shadow.

❀ Circle and write the correct word.

1. There is a _____ in the pine.

   kite   five

2. Let's get a _____ .

   bike   bite

3. There are five rabbits under the _____ .

   nine   pine

4. Let's get a _____ .

   bite   mike

5. There are _____ books under the desk.

   dive   five

✿ Listen and repeat.

ide → h ide → hide

ime → l ime → lime

-ide

h ide   hide   r ide   ride

-ime

l ime   lime   t ime   time

✿ Listen and repeat.

ipe → p ‧ ipe → pipe

ire → f ‧ ire → fire

-ipe

p ipe pipe

w ipe wipe

-ire

f ire fire

t ire tire

Chant Along!

✿ Listen and circle the correct picture and the rhyme.

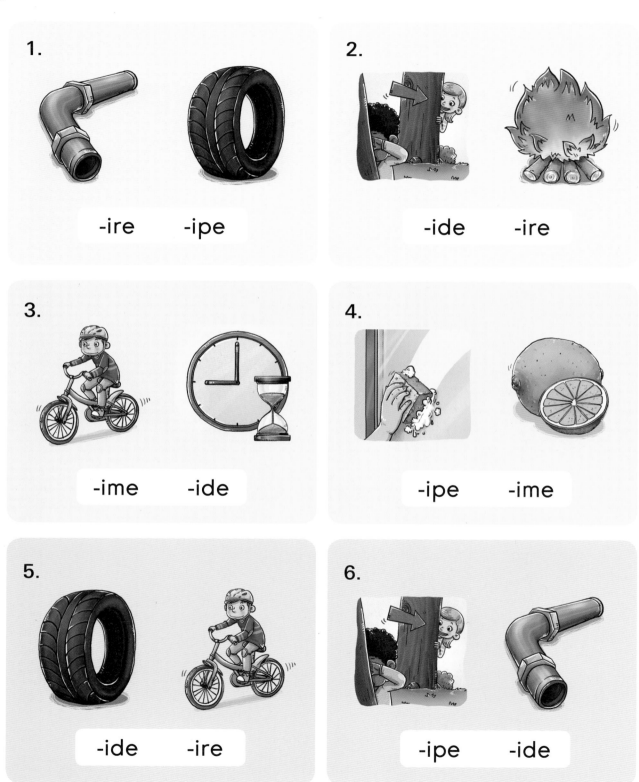

1.

-ire   -ipe

2.

-ide   -ire

3.

-ime   -ide

4.

-ipe   -ime

5.

-ide   -ire

6.

-ipe   -ide

❊ Check the rhyme and write the word.

1. ☐ ide ☐ ire

   f _____

2. ☐ ipe ☐ ime

   p _____

3. ☐ ire ☐ ipe

   t _____

4. ☐ ipe ☐ ide

   h _____

5. ☐ ime ☐ ide

   t _____

✿ Match the pictures with the same ending sound.
Then write.

1.  • •

2.  • •

3.  • •

4.  • •

✿ Listen and circle the word. Then match.

1. fire
time
•

2. tire
wipe
•

3. lime
hide
•

4. pipe
ride
•

✿ Write the missing letters. Then fill in the puzzle.

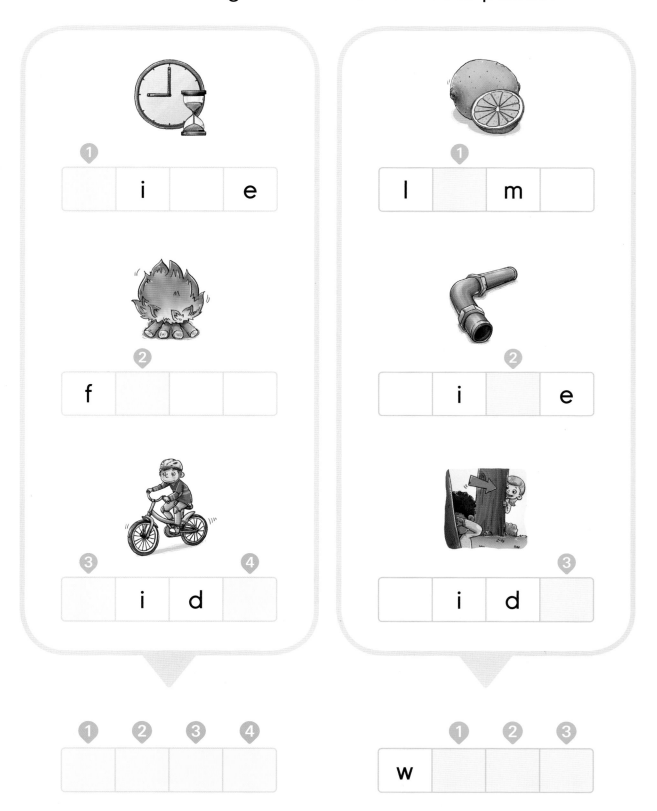

1. [ ] i [ ] e

2. f [ ] [ ] [ ]

3. [ ] i d [ ] 4.

1. l [ ] m [ ]

2. [ ] i [ ] e

3. [ ] i d [ ]

1 2 3 4
[ ] [ ] [ ] [ ]

1 2 3
w [ ] [ ] [ ]

I wipe ⬛ a pipe.

I wipe a tire ⬤ .

The bike is clean.

Dad rides 🚲 a bike.

We hide ⬛ behind limes.

> • Place the sticker on the shadow.

❀ Circle and write the correct word.

1. I wipe a _____ .

   pipe   time

2. We _____ a bike.

   hide   ride

3. I _____ behind a car.

   lime   hide

4. I _____ a lime.

   lime   wipe

5. Cats hide behind a _____ .

   fire   tire

✿ Match the picture with the correct letters.

1.  •   • -ire

2.  •   • -ase

3.  •   • -ape

4.  •   • -ike

5.  •   • -ave

6. •   • -ate

7.  •   • -ite

8.  •   • -ipe

9.  •   • -ime

10.  •   • -ame

❊ Listen and circle the picture.

1.

2.

3.

4.

❊ Listen and write the missing letters.

1.

c __ p __

2.

f __ r __

3.

d __ t __

4.

__ i __ e

5.

__ a __ e

6.

__ i __ e

✿ Match and write the word.

1.

c •
• ape
• age

_____
_____
_____

2.

c •
• ave
• ate

_____
_____
_____

3.

p •
• ine
• ime

_____
_____
_____

4.

h •
• ide
• ike

_____
_____
_____

5.

c •
• ive
• ase

_____
_____
_____

6.

k •
• ite
• ane

_____
_____
_____

Listen and circle. Then answer the question.

How many did you circle?

vase: _____   lime: _____   cape: _____

❀ Listen and repeat.

ose → n · ose → nose

-ose

n ose   nose

h ose   hose

p ose   pose

r ose   rose

✿ Listen and repeat.

ole → h ole → hole

ope → r ope → rope

-ole

h ole   hole

p ole   pole

-ope

r ope   rope

h ope   hope

Chant Along!

❋ Listen and circle the picture.

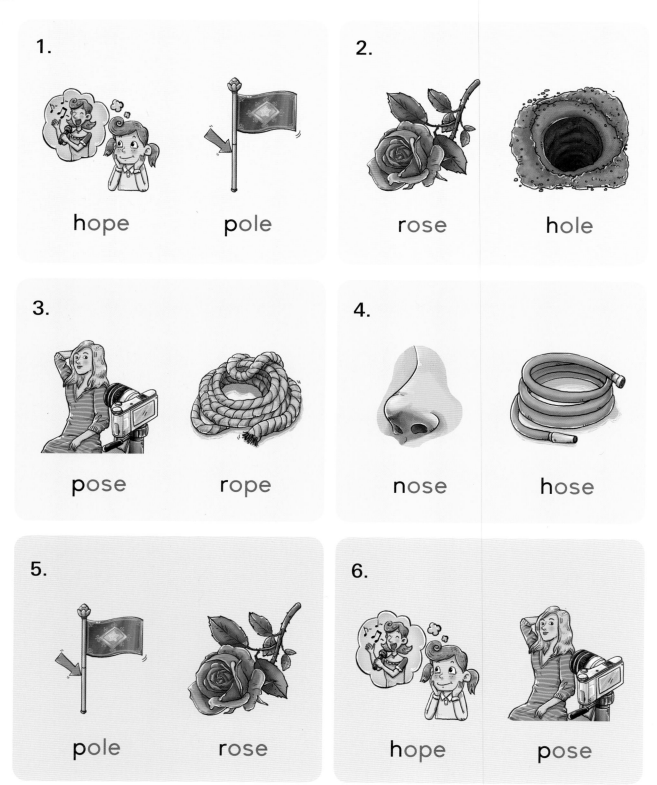

1.

hope   pole

2.

rose   hole

3.

pose   rope

4.

nose   hose

5.

pole   rose

6.

hope   pose

✿ Listen and match.

1.

h

⊐ ole

⊐ ose

2.

p

⊐ ole

⊐ ope

3.

r

⊐ ope

⊐ ose

4.

r

⊐ ole

⊐ ope

✿ Circle the correct ending sound. Then complete the word.

1.

ole
ose

h ___ ___ ___

2.

ope
ose

n ___ ___ ___

3.

ope
ole

h ___ ___ ___

4.

ose
ole

p ___ ___ ___

✿ Write the words with the same ending sound.

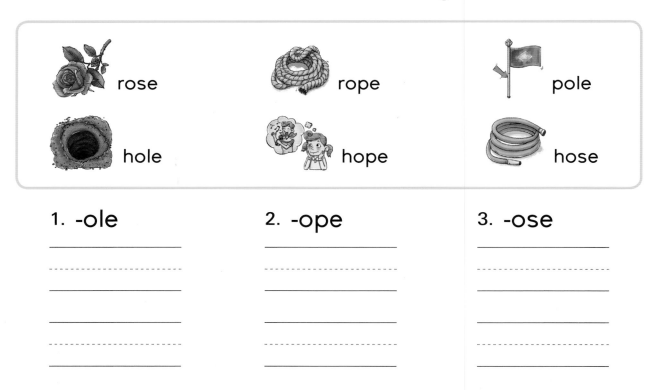

rose   rope   pole

hole   hope   hose

1. -ole

_____

- - - - - - - - - - - - -

_____

_____

- - - - - - - - - - - - -

_____

2. -ope

_____

- - - - - - - - - - - - -

_____

_____

- - - - - - - - - - - - -

_____

3. -ose

_____

- - - - - - - - - - - - -

_____

_____

- - - - - - - - - - - - -

_____

✿ Listen and check the picture. Then circle the word.

1.

c a s n o s e

2.

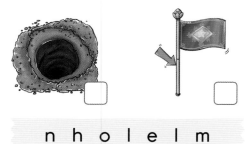

n h o l e l m

3.

r o s r o p e

4.

y e p o s e h

Fill in the puzzle.

I smell a rose with my nose.

Oh! I fall into a hole .

Dad says, "Grab this rope ."

Mom says, "Grab this pole ."

Wow, I come out!

• Place the sticker on the shadow.

✿ Circle and write the correct word.

1. I smell a rose with my _____ .

nose   hope

2. I fall into a _____ .

rope   hole

3. Mom says, "Grab this _____ ."

hose   pole

4. Dad says, "Grab this _____ ."

pose   rope

5. Dad smells a _____ with his nose.

rose   pole

e-learning   game   **Unit 5 · 49**

❀ Listen and repeat.

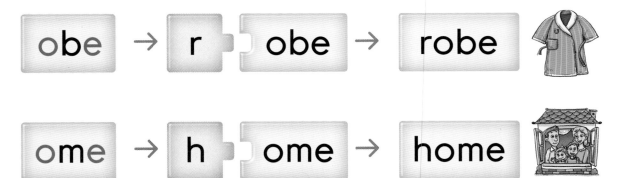

obe → r obe → robe

ome → h ome → home

-obe

r obe   robe   gl obe   globe

-ome

h ome   home   d ome   dome

✿ Listen and repeat.

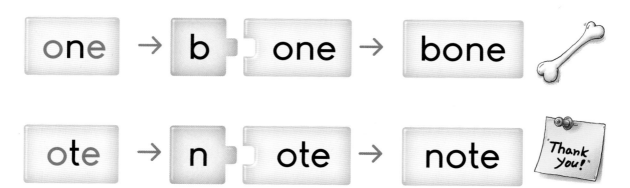

Chant Along!

✿ Listen and circle the picture.

1.

cone   home

2.

note   globe

3.

home   robe

4.

vote   dome

5.

globe   bone

6.

robe   note

✾ Listen and match.

1.
r

obe

one

2.
d

ome

ote

3.
v

obe

ote

4.
c

one

ome

✾ Circle the correct ending sound. Then complete the word.

1.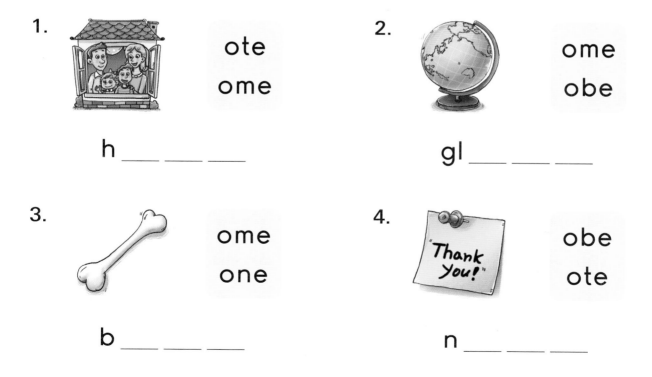
ote
ome

h ___ ___ ___

2.
ome
obe

gl ___ ___ ___

3.
ome
one

b ___ ___ ___

4.
obe
ote

n ___ ___ ___

✿ Write the words with the same ending sound.

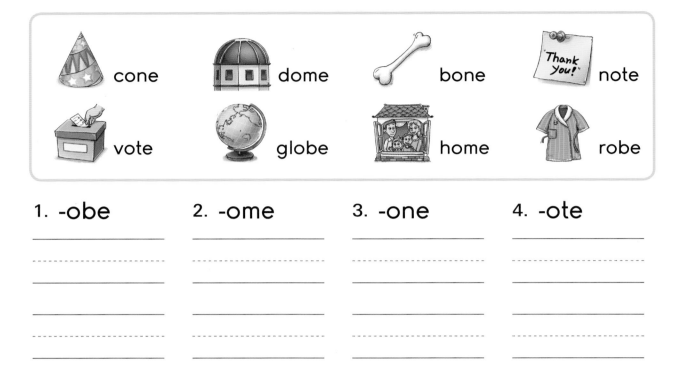

cone dome bone note

vote globe home robe

1. -obe

2. -ome

3. -one

4. -ote

 ✿ Listen and check the picture. Then circle the word.

1.

d b o n e m e

2.

i g l o b e k

3.

h o m e d o m

4.

l a s n o t e

✿ Write the correct word under each picture.

globe   cone   home   bone   note   robe

I make a robe.

It is my cat's robe.

I make a dome.

It is my cat's home.

I write her name on a note.

• Place the sticker on the shadow.

✿ Circle and write the correct word.

1. I make a _____ .

   robe   globe

2. I write her name on a _____ .

   bone   note

3. We make a _____ .

   globe   dome

4. I write my name on a _____ .

   cone   vote

5. This is my cat's _____ .

   home   robe

✿ Listen and repeat.

une → d une → dune

-une

d une → dune

J une → June

t une → tune

✽ Listen and repeat.

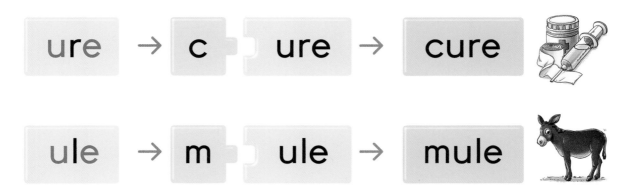

-ure

c ure   cure

p ure   pure

-ule

m ule   mule

Chant Along!

✿ Listen and circle the picture. Then match.

1.

-ule   -une

2.

-ure   -une

3.

-ule   -ure

4.

-ure   -une

5.

-une   -ure

6.

-une   -ule

✿ Circle the correct ending sound. Then complete the word.

1.

une
ule

d _____ _____ _____

2.

une
ure

c _____ _____ _____

3.

ule
ure

m _____ _____ _____

4.

ure
une

J _____ _____ _____

5.

ure
ule

p _____ _____ _____

6.

ule
une

t _____ _____ _____

❋ Write the rhyme and the word.

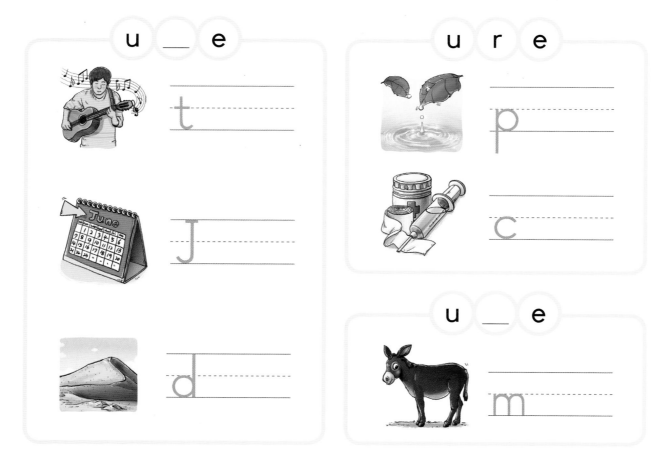

u __ e

t

J

d

u r e

p

c

u __ e

m

❋ Listen and write the missing letters. Then match.

1. __ u __ e   2. __ u __ e   3. __ u __ e   4. __ u __ e

✻ Find and circle the word in the puzzle. Then write the word.

1.

_____

tune

2.

_____

3.

_____

4.

_____

5.

_____

6.

_____

n	m	i	x	J	o	q
t	u	n	e	u	b	c
a	l	d	u	n	e	u
c	e	g	p	e	f	r
p	u	r	e	Y	a	e

It is June .

A mule is on the dune.

He is thirsty.

He hears a sweet tune .

He follows the tune.

He finds a lake.

The water is pure .

• Place the sticker on the shadow.

✿ Circle and write the correct word.

1. It is _____ .

June tune

2. A _____ is thirsty.

dune mule

3. A mule follows the _____ .

tune cure

4. The water is _____ .

mule pure

5. A pipe is on the _____ .

June dune

e-learning   game   Unit 7 · 65

❉ Listen and repeat.

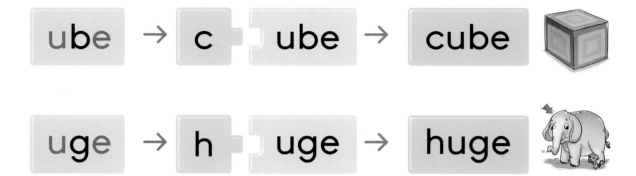

ube → c ube → cube

uge → h uge → huge

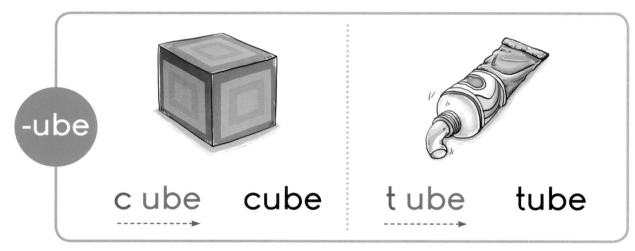

-ube

c ube   cube

t ube   tube

-uge

h uge   huge

✾ Listen and repeat.

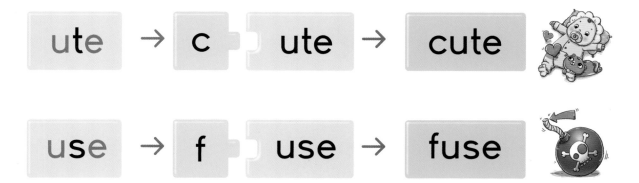

ute → c ute → cute

use → f use → fuse

-ute

c ute   cute   m ute   mute

-use

f use   fuse

Chant Along!

✿ Listen and circle the picture. Then match.

1.

-use   -ube

2.

-uge   -ute

3.

-ute   -ube

4.

-ute   -ube

5.

-ute   -use

6.

-ube   -uge

✿ Circle the correct ending sound. Then complete the word.

1.

ute
uge

m ___ ___ ___

2.

use
ube

c ___ ___ ___

3.

ube
use

f ___ ___ ___

4.

ube
uge

t ___ ___ ___

5.

ute
uge

c ___ ___ ___

6.

uge
ube

h ___ ___ ___

❀ Write the rhyme and the word.

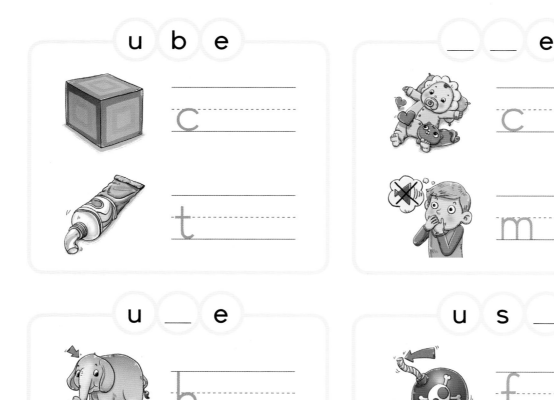

(u)(b)(e)

c ____

t ____

(__)(__)(e)

c ____

m ____

(u)(__)(e)

h ____

(u)(s)(__)

f ____

 ❀ Listen and write the missing letters. Then match.

1.

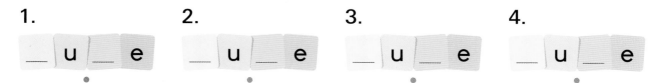

__ u __ e

2.

__ u __ e

3.

__ u __ e

4.

__ u __ e

✿ Write the missing letters. Then fill in the puzzle.

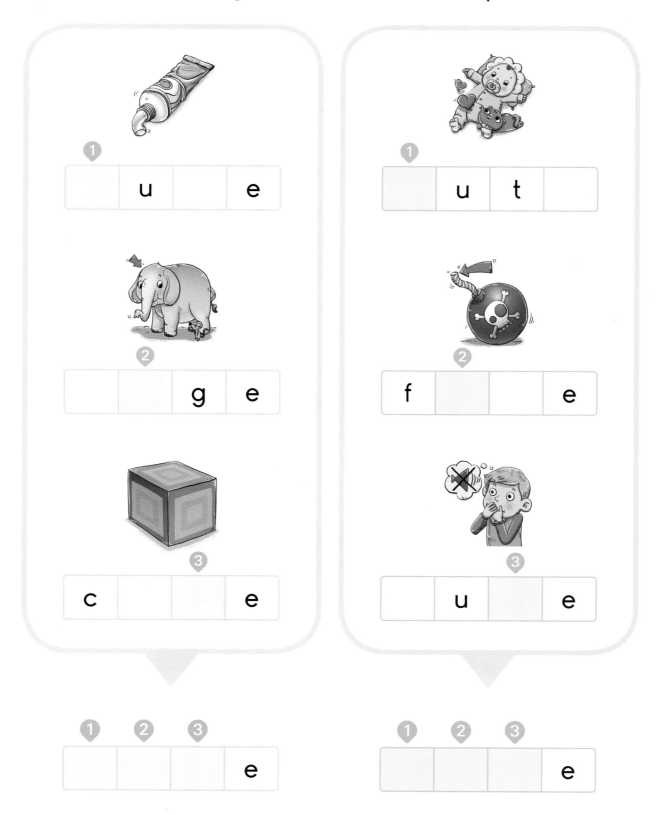

① | u | | e |

② | | g | e |

③ c | | | e |

① | u | t | |

② f | | | e |

③ | u | | e |

① ② ③
| | | e |

① ② ③
| | | e |

Fuse is my dog.

Fuse brings me a cube  .

Fuse brings me a tube .

Woof! Woof!

He wants to play with me.

Fuse is cute .

• Place the sticker on the shadow.

❉ Circle and write the correct word.

1. Fuse is _____ .

   mute   cute

2. Fuse brings me a _____ .

   cute   cube

3. Fuse brings me a _____ .

   fuse   tube

4. My dog is _____ .

   tube   cute

5. The dog is _____ .

   huge   mute

✿ Match the picture with the correct letters.

1.  • • -une

2.  • • -ose

3.  • • -obe

4.  • • -ope

5.  • • -ube

6.  • • -one

7.  • • -une

8.  • • -ute

9.  • • -ome

10.  • • -ote

* Listen and circle the picture.

1.

2.

3.

4.

* Listen and write the missing letters.

1.

h __ g __

2.

n __ t __

3.

r __ s __

4.

__ u __ e

5.

__ o __ e

6.

__ o __ e

✿ Match and write the word.

1.

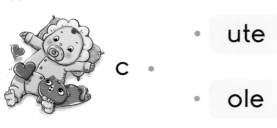

c •

• ute

• ole

_____

_____

2.

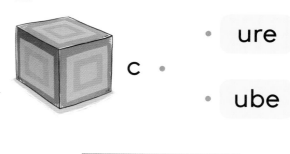

c •

• ure

• ube

_____

_____

3.

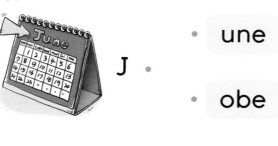

J •

• une

• obe

_____

_____

4.

h •

• ose

• ome

_____

_____

5.

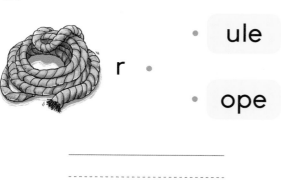

r •

• ule

• ope

_____

_____

6.

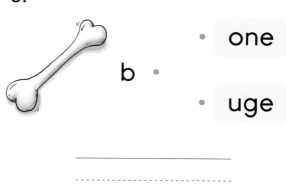

b •

• one

• uge

_____

_____

Listen and connect the words. Then answer the question.

How many words did you connect? _____

✿ Listen to the three words and circle the pictures.

1.

2.

3.

4.

✿ Listen and check the word.

1. cage ☐
   cave ☐

2. cone ☐
   cane ☐

3. June ☐
   nine ☐

4. date ☐
   dune ☐

5. kite ☐
   cute ☐

6. note ☐
   lane ☐

7. pine ☐
   pole ☐

8. huge ☐
   fuse ☐

9. hide ☐
   hose ☐

10. wave ☐
    wipe ☐

✻ Circle and write the word.

k r i s t i m e w n o s e a k e b a k e

1.

_____
- - - - - - - - - - - - - - -
_____

2.

_____
- - - - - - - - - - - - - - -
_____

3.

_____
- - - - - - - - - - - - - - -
_____

t a n c a s e y h o p e u w i p e n a f

4.

_____
- - - - - - - - - - - - - - -
_____

5.

_____
- - - - - - - - - - - - - - -
_____

6.

_____
- - - - - - - - - - - - - - -
_____

n o k i t e j a k i v o t e l g a m e r

7.

_____
- - - - - - - - - - - - - - -
_____

8.

_____
- - - - - - - - - - - - - - -
_____

9.

_____
- - - - - - - - - - - - - - -
_____

❁ Match the picture and the sentence.

1.    •   • There is a kite in the pine.

2.    •   • A mule follows the tune.

3.    •   • I wipe a pipe.

4.    •   • My dog is cute.

5.    •   • I put a cake in a case.

6.    •   • I smell a rose with my nose.

Let's Play!

✿ Roll a die and say a word with the ending sound.

START →

-ike -ote -ire

Skip your next turn.

-une

-age

Go to START

-ure

-ase

-use -ane -ube -one -ite

-ive -ide

FINISH

Listen and check the correct number for the picture.

1.

2.

3.

4.

5.

6.

7.

8.

9.

10.

❋ Write the missing letters.

11.

b ☐ k ☐

12.

t ☐ n ☐

13.

☐ u ☐ e

14.

☐ a ☐ e

15.

☐ o ☐ e

16.

☐ a ☐ e

17.

h ☐ ☐ e

18.

d ☐ ☐ e

19.

t ☐ ☐ e

20.

n ☐ ☐ e

Period	Unit	Target Sounds	Target Words
1	**Unit 1**	age, ake, ase, ate	cage, page, bake, cake, case, vase, date, gate
2			
3	**Unit 2**	ame, ane, ape, ave	game, name, cane, lane, tape, cape, cave, wave
4			
5	**Unit 3**	ike, ine, ite, ive	bike, mike, pine, nine, bite, kite, dive, five
6			
7	**Unit 4**	ide, ime, ipe, ire	hide, ride, lime, time, pipe, wipe, fire, tire
8			
9	**Review 1**	Long vowel a, i	
10	**Unit 5**	ose, ole, ope	nose, hose, pose, rose, hole, pole, rope, hope
11			
12	**Unit 6**	obe, ome, one, ote	robe, globe, home, dome, bone, cone, note, vote
13			
14	**Unit 7**	une, ure, ule	dune, June, tune, cure, pure, mule
15			
16	**Unit 8**	ube, uge, ute, use	cube, tube, huge, cute, mute, fuse
17			
18	**Review 2**	Long vowel o, u	
19	**Challenge**	Long vowel a, i, o, u	
20			

ANSWERS

Student Book **Answers**

• Unit 1

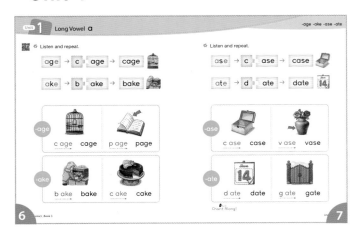

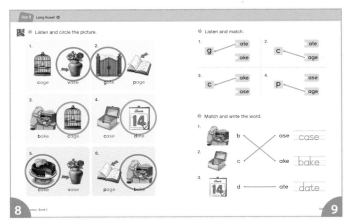

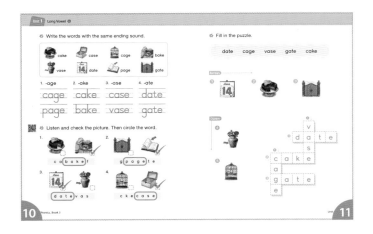

• Unit 2

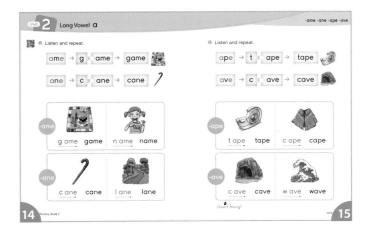

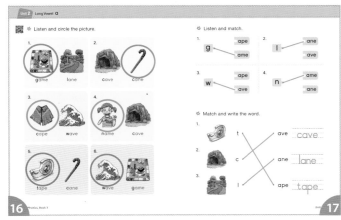

88 · Phonics_Book 3

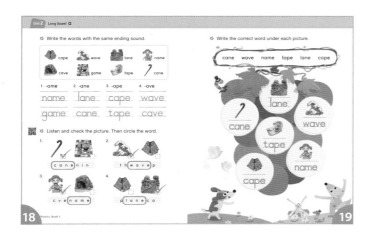

• Unit 3

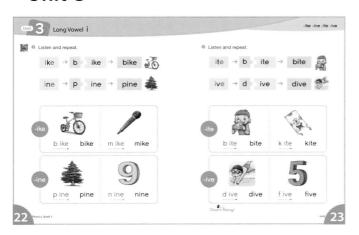

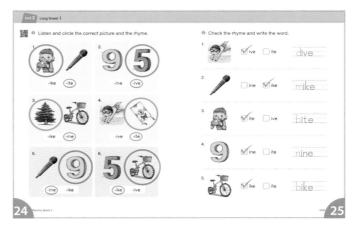

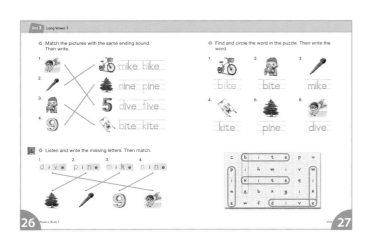

Student Book **Answers**

• Unit 4

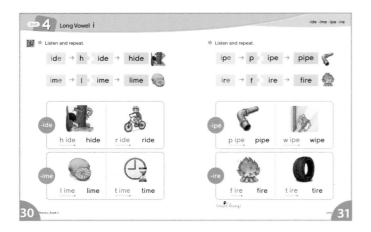

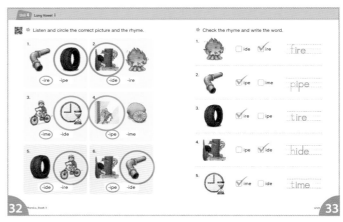

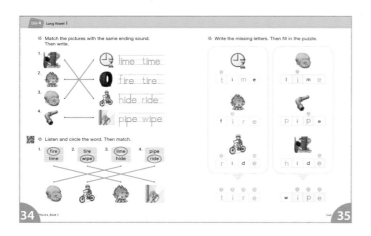

• Review 1

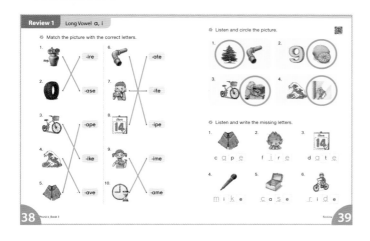

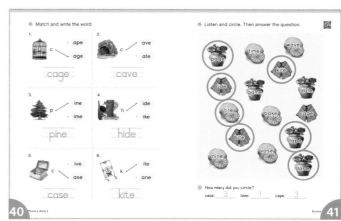

• Unit 5

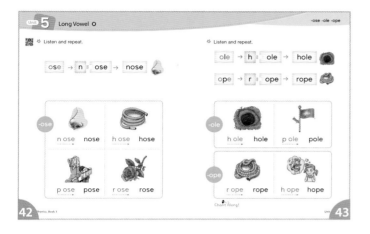

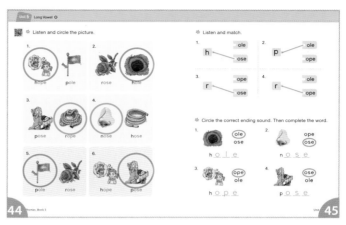

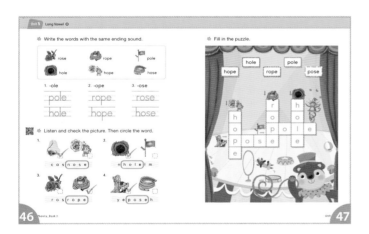

• Unit 6

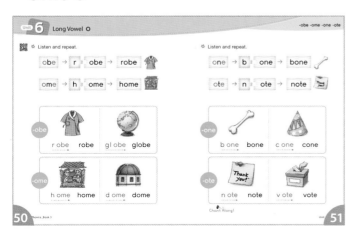

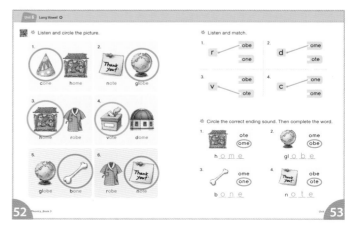

Student Book **Answers**

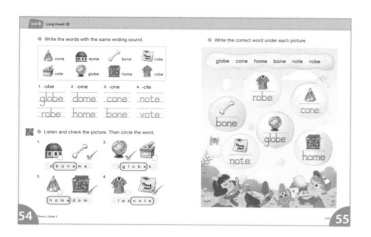

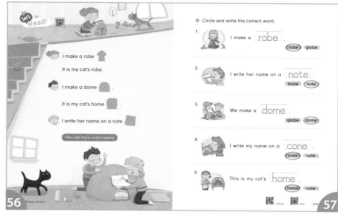

• Unit 7

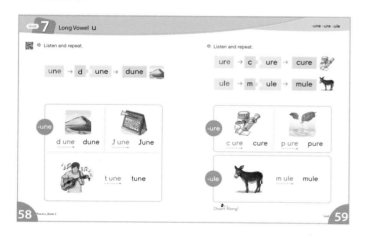

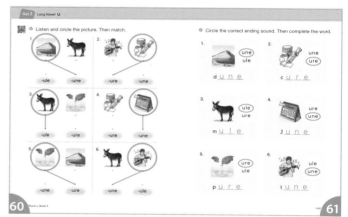

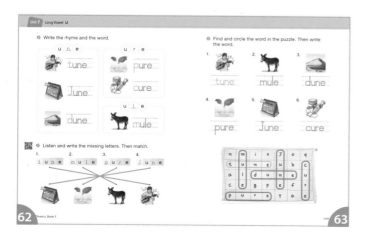

Unit 8

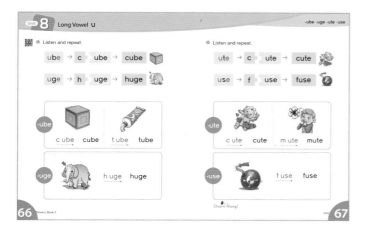

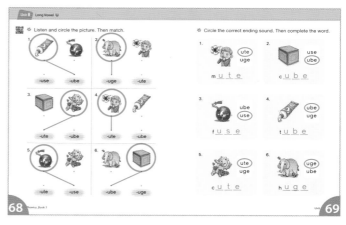

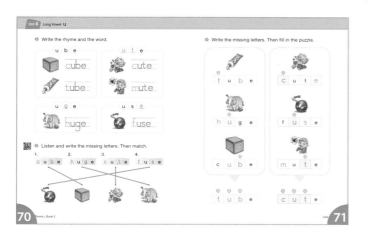

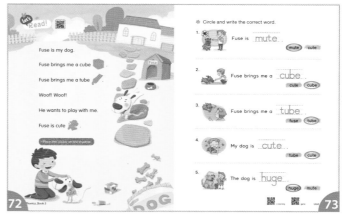

Review 2

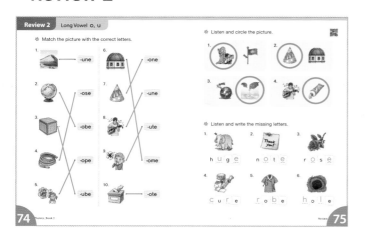

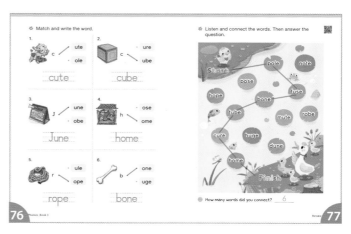

Student Book **Answers**

• Challenge

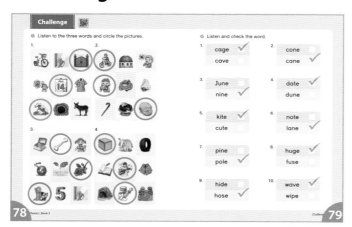

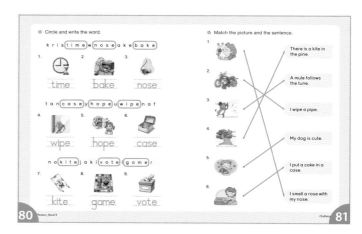

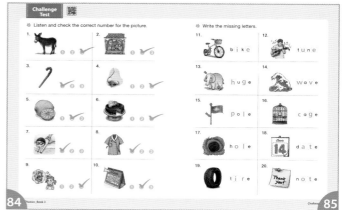

Workbook **Answers**

• Unit 1

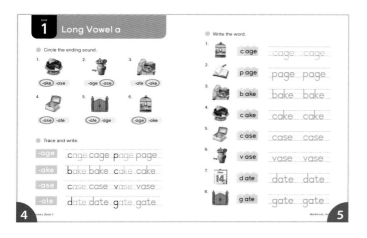

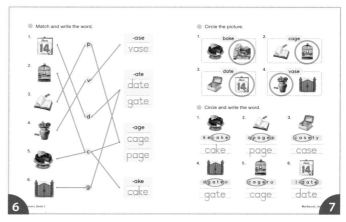

• Unit 2

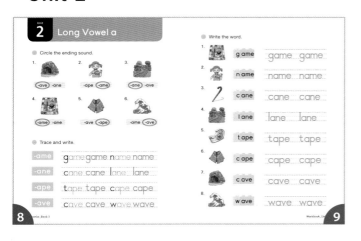

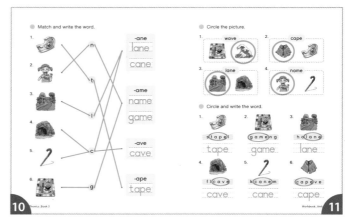

• Unit 3

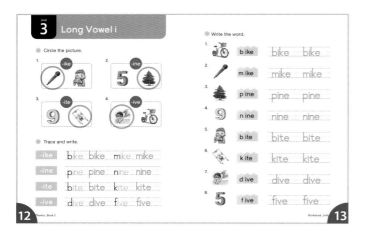

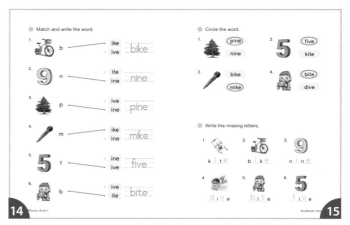

Workbook **Answers**

• Unit 4

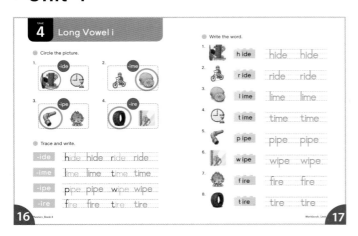

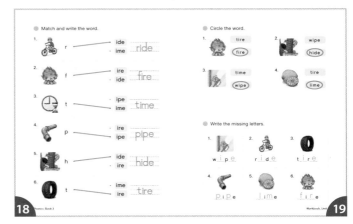

• Review 1

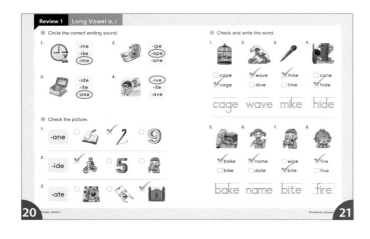

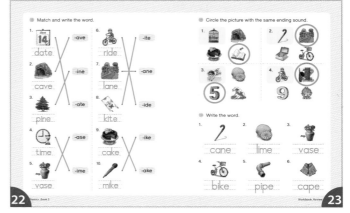

• Unit 5

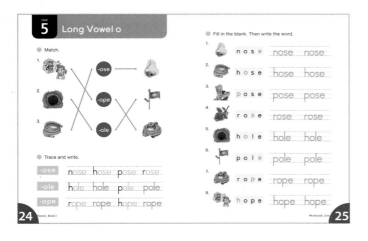

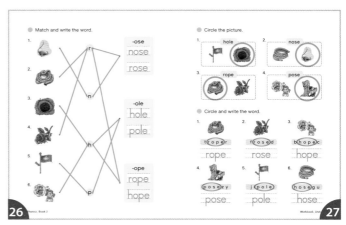

• Unit 6

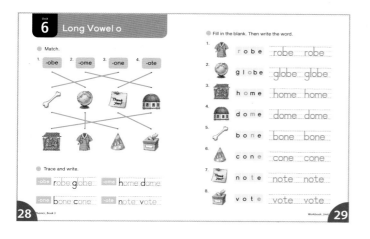

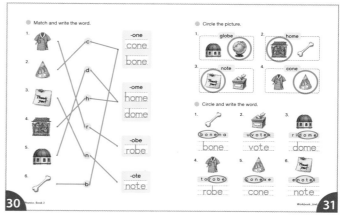

• Unit 7

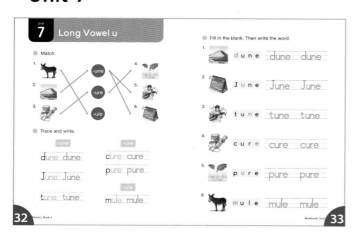

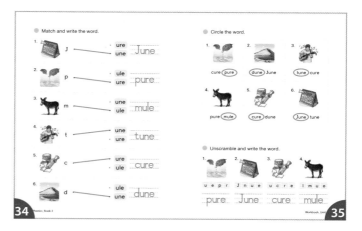

• Unit 8

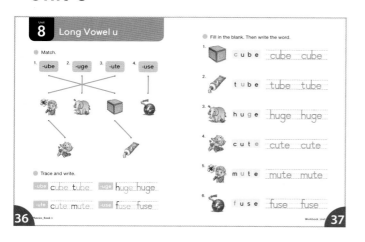

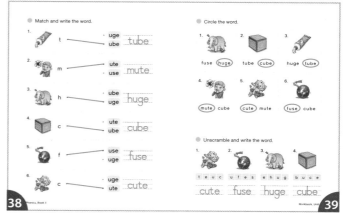

Workbook **Answers**

• Review 2

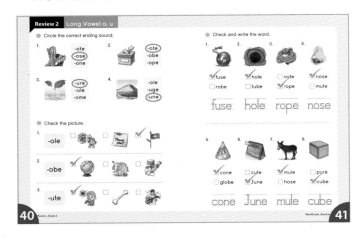

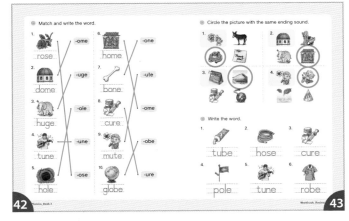

Final Test **Answers**

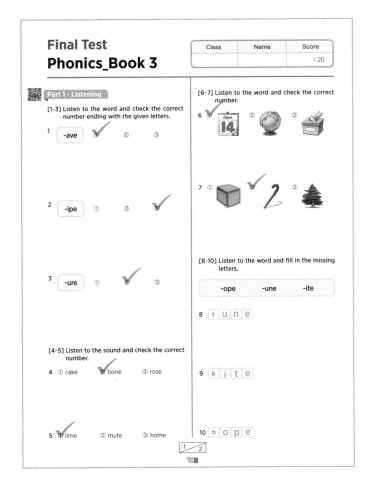

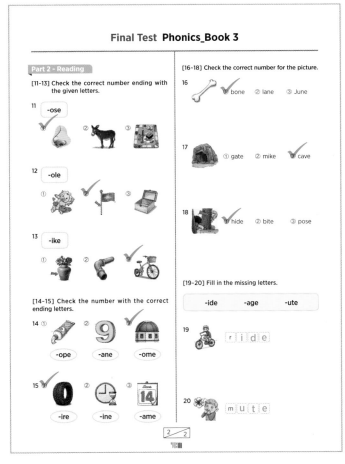

-age

-age

-ake

-ake

-ase

-ase

-ate

-ate

page	cage
cake	bake
vase	case
gate	date

WORD CARDS

-ame

-ame

-ane

-ane

-ape

-ape

-ave

-ave

name	game
lane	cane
cape	tape
wave	cave

WORD CARDS

-ike

-ike

-ine

-ine

-ite

-ite

-ive

-ive

mike	bike
nine	pine
kite	bite
five	dive

-ide

-ide

-ime

-ime

-ipe

-ipe

-ire

-ire

ride	hide
time	lime
wipe	pipe
tire	fire

-ose

-ose

-ose

-ose

-ole

-ole

-ope

-ope

hose	nose
rose	pose
pole	hole
hope	rope

-obe

-obe

-ome

-ome

-one

-one

-ote

-ote

globe	robe
dome	home
cone	bone
vote	note

WORD CARDS

-une

-une

-une

-ure

-ure

-ule

-ube

-ube

June	dune
cure	tune
mule	pure
tube	cube

-uge

-ute

-ute

-use

Excellent!

Good job!

Great!

Wonderful!

cute	huge
fuse	mute

Unit 1
p.12

Unit 2
p.20

Unit 3
p.28

Unit 4
p.36

Unit 5
p.48

Unit 6
p.56

Unit 7
p.64

Unit 8
p.72

BOOK
3

PHONICS
LAND

Long Vowels

WORKBOOK

YBM

PHONICS **LAND**

BOOK **3**

Long Vowels

WORKBOOK

YBM

Contents

🌀 Circle the ending sound.

1.

-ake   -ase

2.

-age   -ase

3.

-ate   -ake

4.

-ase   -ate

5.

-ate   -age

6.

-age   -ake

🌀 Trace and write.

-age	cage	page
-ake	bake	cake
-ase	case	vase
-ate	date	gate

○ Write the word.

1. c age   *cage*   *cage*

2. p age

3. b ake

4. c ake

5. c ase

6. v ase

7. d ate

8. g ate

Match and write the word.

1.

p

-ase
_____

2.

v

-ate
_____

3.

d

4.

-age
_____

5.

c

6.

g

-ake
_____

Circle the picture.

1. bake

2. cage

3. date

4. vase

Circle and write the word.

1.

k e c a k e

_____

2.

q p a g e p

_____

3.

c a s e t y

_____

4.

d g a t e o

_____

5.

c a g e r u

_____

6.

l i d a t e

_____

Long Vowel a

🌀 Circle the ending sound.

1.

-ave   -ane

2.

-ape   -ame

3.

-ane   -ave

4.

-ame   -ane

5.

-ave   -ape

6.

-ame   -ave

🌀 Trace and write.

-ame	game	name
-ane	cane	lane
-ape	tape	cape
-ave	cave	wave

Write the word.

1. g ame _____

2. n ame _____

3. c ane _____

4. l ane _____

5. t ape _____

6. c ape _____

7. c ave _____

8. w ave _____

Match and write the word.

1.

n

-ane

2.

t

3.

l

-ame

4.

5.

c

-ave

6.

g

-ape

Circle the picture.

1. wave

2. cape

3. lane

4. name

Circle and write the word.

1. s t a p e l

_____

2. g a m e n g

_____

3. h o l a n e

_____

4. f l c a v e

_____

5. k c a n e m

_____

6. c a p e v e

_____

Long Vowel i

◎ Circle the picture.

1.
-ike

2.
-ine

3.
-ite

4.
-ive

◎ Trace and write.

-ike	bike	mike
-ine	pine	nine
-ite	bite	kite
-ive	dive	five

Write the word.

1. b ike _____

2. m ike _____

3. p ine _____

4. n ine _____

5. b ite _____

6. k ite _____

7. d ive _____

8. f ive _____

Match and write the word.

1. b •
   • ike _____
   • ive _____

2. n •
   • ite _____
   • ine _____

3. p •
   • ive _____
   • ine _____

4. m •
   • ike _____
   • ine _____

5. f •
   • ine _____
   • ive _____

6. b •
   • ive _____
   • ite _____

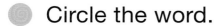 Circle the word.

1. pine

   nine

2.  five

   kite

3. bike

   mike

4. five

   bite

   dive

Write the missing letters.

1. k _ t _

2.  b _ k _

3. n _ n _

4.  _ i _ e

5.  _ i _ e

6. _ i _ e

◎ Circle the picture.

1.

-ide

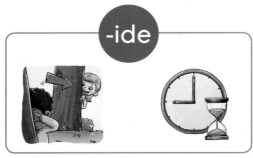

2.

-ime

3.

-ipe

4.

-ire

◎ Trace and write.

-ide	hide	ride
-ime	lime	time
-ipe	pipe	wipe
-ire	fire	tire

Write the word.

1. h ide

2. r ide

3. l ime

4. t ime

5. p ipe

6. w ipe

7. f ire

8. t ire

Match and write the word.

1. r •
   • ide ——————
   • ime ——————

2. f •
   • ire ——————
   • ide ——————

3. t •
   • ipe ——————
   • ime ——————

4. p •
   • ire ——————
   • ipe ——————

5. h •
   • ide ——————
   • ire ——————

6. t •
   • ime ——————
   • ire ——————

● Circle the word.

1. tire / fire

2. wipe / hide

3. time / wipe

4. tire / lime

● Write the missing letters.

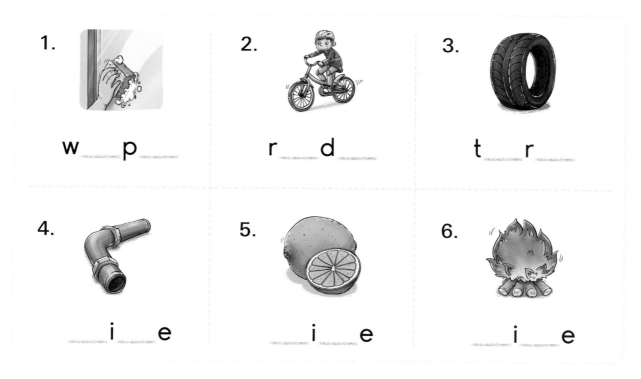

1. w __ p __

2. r __ d __

3. t __ r __

4. __ i __ e

5. __ i __ e

6. __ i __ e

◎ Circle the correct ending sound.

1.

-ine
-ike
-ime

2.

-ipe
-ape
-ane

3.

-ide
-ite
-ase

4.

-ive
-ite
-ave

◎ Check the picture.

1.
 -ane
☐   ☐   ☐

2.
 -ide
☐   ☐   ☐

3.
 -ate
☐   ☐    ☐

Check and write the word.

1.
☐ cape
☐ cage

_____

2.
☐ wave
☐ dive

_____

3.
☐ mike
☐ lime

_____

4.
☐ cane
☐ hide

_____

5.
☐ bake
☐ bike

_____

6.
☐ name
☐ date

_____

7.
☐ wipe
☐ bite

_____

8.
☐ fire
☐ five

_____

Match and write the word.

1. -ave

2. -ine

3. -ate

4. -ase

5. -ime

6. -ite

7. -ane

8. -ide

9. -ike

10. -ake

Circle the picture with the same ending sound.

1.

2.

3.
5

4.
9

Write the word.

1.
_____
- - - - - - - - - - -
_____

2.
_____
- - - - - - - - - - -
_____

3.
_____
- - - - - - - - - - -
_____

4.
_____
- - - - - - - - - - -
_____

5.
_____
- - - - - - - - - - -
_____

6.
_____
- - - - - - - - - - -
_____

Match.

1.  • • -ose • •

2.  • • -ope • •

3.  • • -ole • •

Trace and write.

-ose	nose hose pose rose
-ole	hole pole
-ope	rope hope

Fill in the blank. Then write the word.

1. | n | o | s | e |

2. | h | | s | e |

3. | | o | s | e |

4. | r | o | | e |

5. | h | | l | e |

6. | p | o | l | |

7. | r | o | | e |

8. | | o | p | e |

Match and write the word.

1.

r

-ose

2.

3.

n

-ole

4.

h

5.

-ope

6.

p

Circle the picture.

1.
hole
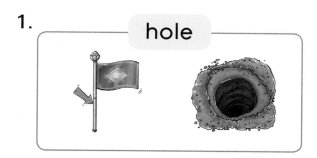

2.
nose
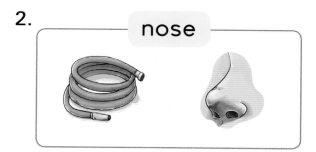

3.
rope

4.
pose

 Circle and write the word.

1.

t r o p e r

_____

2.

f r o s e d

_____

3.

b h o p e c

_____

4.

p o s e z y

_____

5.

j i p o l e

_____

6.

h o s e g u

_____

 Match.

1. -obe   2. -ome   3. -one   4. -ote

 Trace and write.

-obe    -ome

-one    -ote note vote

Fill in the blank. Then write the word.

1. o b e _____

2. g l _ b e _____

3. h _ m e _____

4. d o _ e _____

5. b o _ e _____

6. c o n _ _____

7. n o _ e _____

8. v o t _ _____

◎ Match and write the word.

1.

        •   c

                            -one

2.

        •   d

3.

        •   h

                            -ome

4.

        •   r

5.

        •   n

                            -obe

6.

        •   b

                            -ote

Circle the picture.

1.
globe

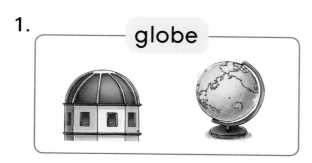

2.
home

3.
note

4.
cone

Circle and write the word.

1.

b o n e n a

_____
- - - - - - - - - - - - - -
_____

2.

u v o t e k

_____
- - - - - - - - - - - - - -
_____

3.

r i d o m e

_____
- - - - - - - - - - - - - -
_____

4.

t o r o b e

_____
- - - - - - - - - - - - - -
_____

5.

c o n e x e

_____
- - - - - - - - - - - - - -
_____

6.

e n o t e i

_____
- - - - - - - - - - - - - -
_____

Long Vowel u

◎ Match.

1. •   -une •   • 4.

2. •   -ure •   • 5.

3. •   -ule •   • 6.

◎ Trace and write.

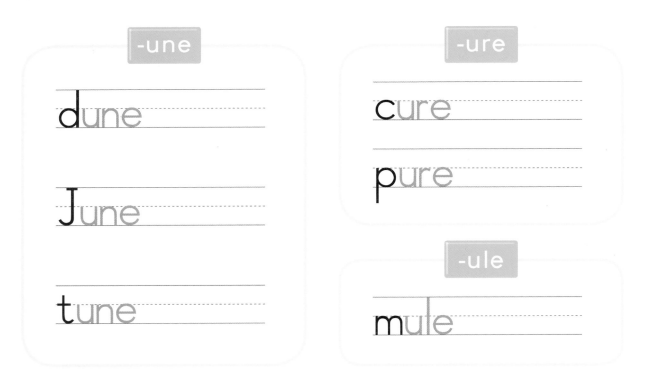

-une

dune

June

tune

-ure

cure

pure

-ule

mule

Fill in the blank. Then write the word.

1. d **u n e** _____

2. **J** u **n e** _____

3. **t u** n **e** _____

4. **c u r** e _____

5. **p** u **r e** _____

6. m **u l e** _____

Match and write the word.

1. J •
   • ure —————
   • une —————

2. p •
   • ule —————
   • ure —————

3. m •
   • une —————
   • ule —————

4. t •
   • une —————
   • ure —————

5. c •
   • ure —————
   • ule —————

6. d •
   • ule —————
   • une —————

Circle the word.

1.

cure   pure

2.

dune   June

3.

tune   cure

4.

pure   mule

5.

cure   dune

6.

June   tune

Unscramble and write the word.

1.

u e p r

_____

2.

J n u e

_____

3.

u c r e

_____

4.

l m u e

_____

 Match.

1. -ube   2. -uge   3. -ute   4. -use

Trace and write.

-ube	cube tube	-uge	huge
-ute	cute mute	-use	fuse

Fill in the blank. Then write the word.

1. $\quad$ c $\vert$ u $\vert$ b $\vert$ e

2. $\quad$ t $\vert$ $\quad$ $\vert$ b $\vert$ e

3. $\quad$ h $\vert$ u $\vert$ g $\vert$ e

4. $\quad$ c $\vert$ u $\vert$ t $\vert$ e

5. $\quad$ m $\vert$ u $\vert$ t $\vert$ e

6. $\quad$ f $\vert$ u $\vert$ s $\vert$ e

Match and write the word.

1. t •
   • uge _____
   • ube _ _ _ _ _ _

2. m •
   • ute _____
   • use _ _ _ _ _ _

3. h •
   • ube _____
   • uge _ _ _ _ _ _

4. c •
   • ute _____
   • ube _ _ _ _ _ _

5. f •
   • use _____
   • uge _ _ _ _ _ _

6. c •
   • uge _____
   • ute _ _ _ _ _ _

Circle the word.

1.

fuse   huge

2.

tube   cube

3.

huge   tube

4.

mute   cube

5.

cute   mute

6.

fuse   cube

Unscramble and write the word.

1.

t e u c

_____

2.

u f e s

_____

3.

e h u g

_____

4.

b u c e

_____

◎ Circle the correct ending sound.

1.

-ote
-ose
-one

2.

-ote
-obe
-ope

3.

-ure
-ule
-ome

4.

-ole
-uge
-une

◎ Check the picture.

1. -ole
☐    ☐   ☐

2. -obe
☐    ☐   ☐

3. -ute
☐   ☐    ☐

🌀 Check and write the word.

1.

☐ fuse
☐ robe

_____

2.

☐ hole
☐ tube

_____

3.

☐ note
☐ rope

_____

4.

☐ nose
☐ mute

_____

5.

☐ cone
☐ globe

_____

6.

☐ cute
☐ June

_____

7.

☐ mule
☐ hose

_____

8.

☐ pure
☐ cube

_____

@ Match and write the word.

1. -ome

2. -uge

3. -ole

4. -une

5. -ose

6. -one

7. -ute

8. -ome

9. -obe

10. -ure

◎ Circle the picture with the same ending sound.

1.

2.

3.

4.

◎ Write the word.

1.

_____
- - - - - - - - - - -
_____

2.

_____
- - - - - - - - - - -
_____

3.

_____
- - - - - - - - - - -
_____

4.

_____
- - - - - - - - - - -
_____

5.

_____
- - - - - - - - - - -
_____

6.

_____
- - - - - - - - - - -
_____